W9-BFC-148

The World's Deadliest

The Deadliest Animals on Earth

by Erika L. Shores

Reading Consultant:
Barbara J. Fox
Reading Specialist
North Carolina State University

Content Consultant:
Dwight Lawson, PhD
Senior Vice President: Collections, Education, and Conservation
Zoo Atlanta
Atlanta, Georgia

CAPSTONE PRESS
a capstone imprint

Blazers is published by Capstone Press,
151 Good Counsel Drive, P.O. Box 669, Mankato, Minnesota 56002.
www.capstonepress.com

Printed in the United States of America in Stevens Point, Wisconsin.
092009
005619WZS10

 Books published by Capstone Press are manufactured with paper
containing at least 10 percent post-consumer waste.

Library of Congress Cataloging-in-Publication Data
Shores, Erika L., 1976–
    The deadliest animals on earth / by Erika L. Shores.
        p. cm. — (Blazers. The world's deadliest)
    Includes bibliographical references and index.
    Summary: "Describes deadly animals and what makes them dangerous" — Provided
by publisher.
        ISBN 978-1-4296-3929-3 (library binding)
        1. Dangerous animals — Juvenile literature. I. Title.
QL100.S565 2010
591.6'5 — dc22

                                                                2009028637

Editorial Credits

Abby Czeskleba, editor; Matt Bruning, designer; Svetlana Zhurkin, media researcher;
    Laura Manthe, production specialist

Photo Credits

Alamy/World Pictures, 23
Corbis/Amos Nachoum, 7
Getty Images/National Geographic/Jason Edwards, 29; Stone/James Balog, 9;
    Visuals Unlimited/Brandon Cole, 19
iStockphoto/Nicholas Fallows, 13
Nature Picture Library/Tony Phelps, 25
Peter Arnold/Biosphoto/J.-L. Klein & M.-L. Hubert, 5; Biosphoto/Sylvain Cordier, 15;
    Kelvin Aitken, 21
Shutterstock/Audrey Snider-Bell, cover (grizzly bear); Gerrit de Vries, 16; Marc Dietrich, cover
    (snakeskin texture); Michael Lynch, 26; Verena Lüdemann, 11

The author dedicates this book to her dad, Dick Mikkelson, who shares her love
for animals — wild and tame.

TABLE OF CONTENTS

DEADLY ATTACKS

Deadly animals kill with speed, sharp teeth, and long claws. They attack because they're hungry or feel threatened. People around the world fear these dangerous beasts.

SORT OF DANGEROUS

STINGING TAILS

Watch out for stingrays in shallow ocean water. Their pointy tails sting people and other animals. Sharp spines on the tail release **venom**. A stab to the chest or stomach can be deadly.

DANGER *Meter*

venom – a poisonous liquid made by some animals

HEAVY HITTERS

Never surprise a brown bear. This large mammal will attack if startled. Brown bears' large paws deliver hard blows. They can run faster than people. Brown bears run up to 35 miles (56 kilometers) per hour.

DEADLY FACT

In North America, brown bears are called grizzly bears.

STAY BACK

Hippos will attack when they feel threatened. They use their 1-foot (.3-meter) long teeth to attack people and animals. In Africa, they kill more people than any other animal.

DEADLY FACT

Rhinos and elephants are the only land animals larger than hippos.

THUNDERING HERDS

In India, elephants **trample** hundreds of people to death each year. Hungry elephants enter villages. They crush people who get in their way.

trample – to damage or crush something by walking heavily all over it

Chapter 3

VERY DANGEROUS

DANGER *Meter*

NASTY BITES

Few people survive a run-in with the world's heaviest lizard. Komodo dragons have sharp, jagged teeth. They release venom in their bites. The venom causes animals and people to bleed to death.

ON THE HUNT

Hungry lions prowl through Africa looking for **prey**. Lions in Tanzania attack people when they can't find other animals to eat. Some experts think mother lions teach cubs how to hunt humans.

prey – an animal hunted by another animal for food

SHARK ATTACK

Sharks tear into flesh using rows of razor-sharp teeth. A great white shark can smell blood from 3 miles (4.8 kilometers) away. Great whites attack about 50 people each year.

DEADLY FACT

Great white sharks have up to 300 teeth.

SWIMMERS BEWARE

In Australia, swimmers who brush up against a box jellyfish are in trouble. A sting delivers enough venom to kill a person in minutes.

DEADLY *FACT*

Pour vinegar on a sting from a box jellyfish. Vinegar stops the venom from spreading.

Chapter 4

EXTREMELY DANGEROUS

CRUSHING JAWS

DANGER Meter

Saltwater crocodiles leap from the water to grab prey. They wait underwater for the right time to attack. Their powerful bites make it almost impossible to escape.

VICIOUS VIPERS

Saw-scaled viper bites cause **victims** to bleed to death. These snakes kill more people in Africa and Asia than any other snake.

victim – a person who is hurt or killed

amphibian – a cold-blooded animal with a backbone

DON'T TOUCH

Poison dart frogs are only 2 inches (5.1 centimeters) long. But the poison on this tiny **amphibian's** skin is deadly. People can die if the poison gets into a cut. The frog's poison also kills animals.

DEADLY FACT

One frog's poison is strong enough to kill 10 to 20 people.

TAIPAN TERROR

The inland taipan lives in Australia. It is the most venomous snake on land and can kill in seconds. The deadliest animals aren't always out to kill people. But these fierce **predators** will defend themselves.

DEADLY FACT

The venom in an inland taipan's bite can kill 100 people.

predator – an animal that hunts other animals for food

GLOSSARY

amphibian (am-FI-bee-uhn) — a cold-blooded animal with a backbone

cub (KUHB) — a young bear or lion

poison (POI-zuhn) — a substance that can kill or harm someone

predator (PRED-uh-tur) — an animal that hunts other animals for food

prey (PRAY) — an animal hunted by another animal for food

threatened (THRET-uhnd) — frightened or in danger

trample (TRAM-puhl) — to damage or crush something by walking heavily all over it

venom (VEN-uhm) — a poisonous liquid made by some animals

victim (VIK-tuhm) — a person who is hurt or killed

READ MORE

Hansen, Paul. *When Snakes Attack!* When Wild Animals Attack! Berkeley Heights, N.J.: Enslow, 2006.

Jackson, Tom. *Shark Attack.* Crabtree Contact. New York: Crabtree, 2008.

Polydoros, Lori. *Crocodiles: On the Hunt.* Killer Animals. Mankato, Minn.: Capstone Press, 2009.

INTERNET SITES

FactHound offers a safe, fun way to find Internet sites related to this book. All of the sites on FactHound have been researched by our staff.

Here's all you do:

Visit *www.facthound.com*

FactHound will fetch the best sites for you!

INDEX